# The Practical Freelance Writer's Guide to Author Websites

## Build and Manage a Website to Enhance Your Freelance Writing Career

Angela Atkinson

WM Network Books | USA

ISBN 978-0-557-59462-7

Printed in the United States of America.

*"It is impossible to discourage the real writers - they don't give a damn what you say, they're going to write."* ~Sinclair Lewis

\*\*\*

# This book is dedicated to

*My husband, Bill, and our three beautiful children, Cameron, Noah and Sophia. I live and breathe for you and I am so grateful to have you in my life. You have taught me what it means to truly love and be loved without condition.*

*My extended family and friends, particularly those who support me unconditionally both personally and in my career. Without you, I would be nothing. Thank you all, for everything.*

*My friend, partner and fellow co-founder of The WM Network, Alyssa Ast, who talks me down off the ledges of my own neurosis and helps me keep writing every day with her unfailing support. Thank you for always listening and for kicking my butt when I feel like slacking.*

*And finally, to the real writers who follow their dreams and don't give a damn what anyone says. Write on, my friends. Write on.*

The Practical Freelance Writer's Guide to Author Websites

# Table of Contents

# 1

# All About Author Websites

Does every freelance writer need an author website? What if you haven't been published yet? What if you've only published online? How about those old pros with an established list of clients?

These questions have been asked again and again in the freel-ance writing community, and the answer is simple. In the highly-connected society of today, if you want to be (or continue to be) a successful, working writer, you need to have an author web-site.

**What is the purpose of an author site for a freelance writer?**

Most importantly, an author site serves as your own "one stop shop." Think of it like a storefront to which you can direct edi-tors and potential clients to learn about your services. And, correctly implemented, your author site will help sell (yourself and) your services.

As a freelance writer, your author site gives you the opportunity to provide samples of (or links to) your work, an extended bio, contact information and more. It tells your potential clients and/or editors that you mean business--that you're a professional who is committed to your craft.

And, once you begin to establish yourself in your writing career, you can list testimonials, awards, publishing credits and more—all of which, of course, work to your benefit when a client or editor checks you out.

An author site can also help you to establish yourself as an expert in specific niche(s) or topic area(s). You may choose to include an on-site blog or to link to niche or topic related articles, for example.

Plus, a website can take your business to a new level. You won't be limited by local constraints—instead you can take your business worldwide. Many well-fed freelancers work via email, snail mail and phone with clients in other states and even other countries.

And don't forget competition--most working writers these days have their own author sites. To remain competitive, you need an author site too. You want to be a working writer, so do what working writers do—get a website.

## What should be included on a freelance writer's website?

There is no hard and fast formula for success when it comes to author websites for freelancers, but some elements work for nearly any writer who wants to succeed in his career. Of course, you'll want to customize your site to fit your own style and especially your chosen career path and specialty areas.

Here are some basics to consider when creating your site:

**A Dedicated Landing Page**—Serves as a welcome to site visi-tors, and is a good way to briefly introduce yourself and your services.

**An extended biography**—A narrative about you, your writing and publishing career and (briefly) your personal life.

**An author photo**--Ideally, a head shot in which your face can be clearly seen.

**Samples of your work**—Links to and/or text from your previous work.

**Testimonials**—A testimonial from a previous or current client, business associate or fan can go a long way to instill confidence in your abilities for potential clients.

**Services**—A list, detailed enough to be clear, that explains what you can offer your clients.

**A Blog**—Regardless of subject matter, your onsite blog can be another place to showcase your writing skills and keep your site regularly updated.

**Special Projects and Affiliations**—If you own a company, par-ticipate in any writing groups or other professional asso-ciations or are involved with other kinds of writing, or wish to promote a cause or charity, you can include a special page within your website to promote it.

**Awards and Recognitions**—If you receive any sort of award or other type of special recognition for your writing, no matter how small, consider putting it on your website.
**Contact information**—Information on how your potential clients can reach you to obtain a quote or further information about you and/or your services.

Many new writers may find this list intimidating, but it doesn't have to be that way. With a bit of creativity and a good plan of action, even unpublished writers can create a highly successful career-enhancing author website.

In the chapters that follow, each of these page elements will be covered in detail, defining them and offering examples and helpful tips for new writers and their more experienced counterparts.

We'll discuss various webhosting options and their pros and cons. Plus, we'll talk about how to optimize your freelance writer's website for search engines and why you should. Finally, you'll learn how to promote your website. At the back of the book, you'll find a helpful list of resources for freelance writers.

# 2

# Your Dedicated Landing Page

A landing page is the first page a visitor sees when he types your URL into the browser or clicks on your link.

While not every author site has a dedicated landing page, it can add to the allure of your site—and it's an easy way to make a great first impression.

The problem most freelancers run into when it comes to a landing page is deciding what to actually put on the page. After all—if you've done your job right, you've already got everything a potential client needs to know about you and your services in your other pages.

As a freelance writer, you're always selling yourself. So, you can use your landing page as a virtual sales pitch. For example, you might highlight your specialty services, or write a letter to your potential clients explaining what you can do for them.

Alternatively, you might wish to use the landing page as a welcome page. Many freelance writers have created successful landing pages with an informal introduction of themselves and their services, along with a welcome message and a hyperlinked tour of their sites.

In any case, you want to keep your landing page content simple and to the point—don't overwhelm your website visitors with too much flash. Instead, draw them in with your message.

### Tips to Keep Them Reading

**Ensure Continuity**—If you are advertising your services on other websites, even social networking sites, you should consider using the same or a similar headline for your landing page. Most marketing professionals agree that this is a great way to put the site visitor at ease and to increase your perceived credibility.

**Me, Me, Me**—Don't talk about YOU. Talk about what you can do for your potential clients. That means that you should write your landing page copy as though you're speaking directly to a potential client.

**Keep It Simple, Smarty**—As previously mentioned, a successful landing page is simple and to the point. So don't try to get too wordy or fancy—write as you would actually speak to a client. Using a bunch of fifty cent words won't impress anyone, but well-written, easy to read and understand copy will have them eating out of your virtual hand.

**Say What You Gotta**—If you have a lot to say on your landing page, that's ok. But do keep the copy tight and eliminate extra words and phrases. And stick to the point—don't go into a bunch of irrelevant details about you or your personal life on your landing page. That's what your bio is for—so instead, keep the focus on how you can help your potential clients.

**Pointed Placement**—Statistically, most people read headlines, bullet points and, if they like what they see, the beginning and end of the copy on your landing page. So be sure to place the most important points in those positions on your landing page. You can also bold important copy to help it stand out more, but do this sparingly so as not to overwhelm site visitors.

**Remember the Fold**—Try to put your most intriguing information "above the fold," that is, don't require your site visitors to scroll down to see the information that matters. Make your header between 100 and 300 pixels tall to help keep important copy "above the fold."

**Call to Action**—Tell clients exactly what they need to do next. For example, "Click here to request a free quote or to discuss your project."

# 3

# Your Author Bio

While you'll want to have a couple of "short" versions of your author bio for publication with articles and other kinds of freelance writing, you should include an extended author biography on your writer website for a number of reasons.

First, it's often your first introduction to readers and potential clients. Second, a well-written bio can showcase your personali-ty, work ethic, talents, education, accomplishments and more, making you more attractive to potential clients, thus increasing your income potential. And finally, it's simply standard proce-dure for any writer.

## First Person or Third Person?

While there is some debate in the writing community as to

whether it's acceptable to write a bio in the first person, tradition dictates that you write it in the third person. Since a third person bio is appropriate for any writer, it's really the safest bet. While some authors do manage to successfully pull off a first person biography, most well-published writers seem to prefer the third person. This is industry wide—from web writers to journalists to novelists, and everyone in between.

A couple of exceptions to this rule:

- Bio posted in the sidebar of your personal blog
- Any bio posted on social networking profiles

These kinds of bios can be written in the third person, but don't need to be.

## Introducing YOU

Most writers hate writing their own bios. It can feel awkward and unnatural to write about yourself, and you might feel like you're bragging a little when it's time to make note of your ac-accomplishments and abilities.

Even so, a well-written bio can be a major career enhancer, so you've got to move past "bio anxiety" and take control.

Try this brainstorming technique to help get you started. Imagine that your dream client met a friend or business associate of yours, and asked if he knew a good freelance writer. Now, take a moment to consider how you'd want someone else to describe you to that potential client. What would you want a client to know about you and your work? How would you want a friend or business contact to describe your abilities and your work ethic?

These are the kinds of questions that you can answer in your bio. Start brainstorming, and make a list of points you want your clients to know.

### Bios That Work

Though an author bio should be very personalized, many writers aren't sure what kind of information they should include or where to begin. In addition to the ideas you develop during your brainstorming session, you can include a number of elements, depending on your own experiences.

**Education**—If you have a college degree or diploma, specialized training or military experience, include it in your bio. If not, don't focus on it. You don't absolutely need a degree to be a successful freelance writer—you just need to be able to write clearly and effectively and have a handle on grammar, spelling and punctuation. That, combined with a healthy dose of self-esteem, can take you further than a degree alone ever could.

**Writing and Publishing Experience**—If you have published articles, books, blog posts, poems or any other kind of writing, include it in your bio. Don't let a tiny venue make you feel small—tout all of your publishing credits, even if one of them happens to be a website, your local penny saver or a church newsletter. And if you don't have publishing experience? Talk about what you want to write—for example, if you love underwater basket weaving, you can say "Joe Writer enjoys writing about underwater basket weaving and the related subjects." And, if you've written fifteen poems or a yet-to-be-published series on green living on a budget? Include that too. It counts.

**Personal Information**—This is a bit of a gray area, but in general, you don't want to include anything negative about you or your personal life. For example, unless you're selling yourself as a divorce expert, don't mention that you're "happily divorced"— and if you're not covering the weird phobias beat, there's no need to mention your diagnosis of Arachibutyrophobia. (You know, the fear of peanut butter sticking to the roof of your mouth.) Examples of acceptable personal information include a brief description of your family situation (especially if married and/or a parent,) general location of your residence (part of the country, state, county or city—depending on how specific you want to be) and brief statements about your feelings on writing or your career. In some cases, additional personal information may be warranted. For instance, parenting writers may wish to go into more depth on their families and children, as well as their parenting philosophies.

**Hobbies and Interests**—You may mention any hobbies or interests that you have (at least the socially acceptable ones) as potential clients may be looking for a writer with a specific background or skill set (writing related or otherwise.) Generally acceptable examples include things like sports, arts, crafts, parenting—any topic you could talk to your kids about. Unacceptable examples include things like surfing for porn, gossiping like a schoolgirl, littering, excessive sitcom watching—anything you'd be embarrassed if your mother knew. (Of course, there are exceptions for every rule. For example, if you're a Hollywood gossip columnist, owning your chatty habits could be a step in the right direction. Just use your best discretion and consider your intended audience.)

## Professionalism Matters

Skip the IM or text speak. There are no KWIMs or LOLs in professional writing. When you're writing for a professional publication, hoping to get paid, leave that stuff out. Same deal on your author bio. Otherwise, you'll look uneducated and incompetent.

Don't forget to carefully edit your bio, line by line, before publishing it. The fact is that if an editor or potential client reads your bio and finds fifty-seven errors, he not likely to be interested in seeing anything else you have to say (or write.)

### Special Tips for New or Unpublished Writers

As a new writer, you may not feel like you have much to say in a bio—especially if you don't have a college degree or any publishing experience. So what can you do to beef up your bio?

**Get Involved**—If you're not currently involved with a professional association, join one. Sometimes these associations have fees or requirements that can't always be met by brand new writers--so consider joining a local writer's group or an online writing community to start. Now you can say "Ms. Writer is a member of the Camden County Writer's Guild."

**Get Creative**—What are your other areas of expertise? If you're a great tennis player, a gourmet chef or a knitting champion, feel free to say so--but keep it brief, especially if it's not directly related to your work. Something like "Ms. Writer is an award-winning gourmet chef" or "In her spare time, Ms. Writer knits sweaters for the homeless." On the other hand, if you're writing a cookbook, feel free to expand on your love of cooking. You get the idea.

**Think Again**—Take a second look at your publishing credits. Did you write an article for your church or PTA newsletter? Did you publish poetry in college? Even if you've just got an unpublished collection of short stories, you would not be lying if you simply said, "Ms. Writer has written fifteen short stories" or "Ms. Writer enjoys writing short stories."

### About Your Author Pic

Your potential clients want to see what you look like. They feel more comfortable working with someone who has a "face," especially in this day and age when freelancers may never meet their clients in real live, face-to-face encounters.

When you're choosing your author bio photo, choose something that:

**Looks Professional**—Use common sense here. Don't put up a photo of yourself in a bikini on the beach with some dude doing belly shots off your naked torso or that shot from your bache-lor(ette) party with the stripper your friends ordered. Just use a basic, simple and professional looking shot. And if you don't have the money for professional headshots? Remember that a well taken snapshot can appear professional when properly cropped.

**Clearly Shows Your Face**—While a headshot is generally a good choice, some writers like to get a bit more creative. But even if you choose to use a full body shot, be sure that your pho-to is well-lit and that your whole face is clearly visible and not visually obstructed. Otherwise, crop the photo appropriately or choose a different photo.

**Features a Pleasant Expression**—You don't need to be grin-ning from ear-to-ear, but a friendly looking photo will give your clients a more positive feeling about you than a dark scowl. Looking directly into the camera can also make you appear more honest and open.

# Testimonials

Webster's dictionary defines a testimonial as "a statement testifying to benefits received, a character reference or a letter of recommendation."

For your freelance writer's website, testimonials are generally brief comments or statements from colleagues, clients or other people with whom you've worked professionally which effectively endorse you and your services.

Though not every writer chooses to publish testimonials, doing so can offer several benefits.

### Why Testimonials Work

Well-placed testimonials can afford you a certain amount of credibility as a writer. Potential clients and editors who are considering working with you are likely to feel more comfortable doing so if they know that others have had positive experiences. And, through a well-written testimonial, you can let your clients know how incredible you are without having to say so yourself.

Plus, clients who write testimonials on your behalf are statistically very likely to maintain a long term business relationship with you.

### Who to Ask for Testimonials

If you've already had some career success, you can just start with the people you're currently working with (or have worked with in the past.) Include clients, editors and other writers or business owners and community members with whom you've collaborated on projects.

But what if you don't have a long list of clients or colleagues to choose from? Are you just out of luck?

### Finding Testimonials as a New or Unpublished Writer

Get creative. Did you have a favorite teacher in school? Is there a professional friend or family member (with a different last name) who could vouch for your writing ability? Are you involved in an online writing community or writing group?

Can you think of anyone within any of your social networks, "real life" or online that might be willing to help? Any of these would be good places to start when looking for a testimonial.

## How to Ask for a Testimonial

Asking for a testimonial can feel uncomfortable at first, but it is well worth the trouble. The simplest way to get someone to write one for you is to just ask. In general, contact people via the usual method you communicate--so if you typically talk via email, send an email. If you usually speak to the person via phone or in person, do it that way.

Explain what you're looking for (a brief statement regarding the quality of your work, the experience of working with you, etc.) and simply ask for their help. Most people are more than happy to lend a hand, especially because it benefits them as well.

## What's In It for Them

Besides giving them an opportunity to do a good deed, most people are honored to be asked to provide a testimonial. It means that you value their opinion enough to print it on your website. Plus, you can offer link love (i.e. place a link on your site to theirs along with their testimonial.) And, of course, it certainly won't hurt their image.

You can also offer to reciprocate if the situation is appropriate. For example, if one of your clients is a business owner, you could write a testimonial for his page in return for the one he writes for yours. Obviously, offering reciprocation isn't appropriate in every case, so carefully consider the situation before making such an offer.

## Natural Testimonials

As you build your career, clients or readers will send notes or make positive comments about you or your work without being prompted. Usually, this happens informally. Starting now, take note of these compliments. Create a file in which you save each compliment or positive statement about your work, and be sure to note who said what.

You can use these compliments and statements as testimonials. As a courtesy, always ask the person who said or wrote it whether they mind if you post it on your site.

## Keep It Real

One thing to avoid: don't make up testimonials. That doesn't mean that you can't help a well-meaning but writing challenged person to clarify their thoughts. Just don't falsify any statements or say things that just aren't true. You'll not only lose credibility, you could lose potential business too.

# 5

# Services

As a freelance writer, you're more than just a writer. You're a CEO, an accountant, a secretary, a producer of product, a marketing department—and more. You probably do all of your own editing, querying, follow ups, networking, marketing...phone calls, coffee making...the list goes on and on. You're jack of all trades—and a natural multi-tasker.

If you want to be successful freelancer, your website and services offered need to reflect this kind of flexibility.

Obviously, you're a writer. You write because that's what you love to do. And as you create your list of services, you'll want to put writing right on top.

But what happens when you need more business? What other services can freelance writers offer their clients?

Think about all of the things you do for your freelance business. Which things do you enjoy? Which things do people ask you for advice about? Which things do you think other people need help with?

While you run your freelance business, you'll naturally develop other skills, whether through working with your clients or just in producing and promoting your own work. If you develop (or already have) a particular gift for a writing-related service, consider adding it to your list of offered services. Not only can it increase your marketability, but it can increase your overall income.

While every freelance writer is different, here are a few ideas for related services you might consider offering to help increase your income:

- Administrative Support or Representation
- British to American English (and vice versa)
- Business Consulting and/or Coaching (Writing, SEO, newsletters, web content and development, etc)
- Corporate or personal blogging
- Editing
- Ghostwriting

- Marketing
- Mentoring or Coaching Other Writers
- Photography/photojournalism
- Proofreading
- SEO/SEM Services
- Social Networking
- Teaching Classes or Workshops
- Translation
- Website Design and/or Maintenance
- Writing Speeches, Eulogies and Presentations

## Specialty and Niche Services

You can also offer specialty or niche writing, based on your own knowledge and experience. You might include specific genres, topics, kinds of documents (newsletters, whitepapers, brochures, training manuals, etc), press releases, and more. If you take the time to analyze your skills, work history, passions and abilities, you'll see that most everyone can offer some kind of specialty writing.

## Suggested Specialty and Niche Writing Ideas

While this list is certainly not all-inclusive, it may help to spark your creativity when choosing your own specialty and niche writing areas.

- Advertising/Catalog Copy
- Alternative Lifestyles
- Arts
- Babies
- Biographies
- Car Repair, Detailing, etc.
- Computers
- Corporate
- Crafts
- Curriculum
- Decorating
- Direct Mail
- Disabilities & Diseases
- Editorials
- Events
- Family & Parenting
- Flyers, Brochures, Circulars
- Food
- Friendships
- Google (and the related umbrella)
- Greeting Cards

# Services

- Health Insurance
- Holiday Letters
- Home Repair and Modifications
- Homeschooling
- How-to
- Kids
- Law of Attraction
- Linux
- Local Area
- Local/National Bands
- Medical
- Men
- Menus
- Microsoft
- Mobile Phones/Apps
- Music
- Obituaries
- Pet Grooming
- Pet Health
- Pets
- Psychology/Psychiatry
- Recipes
- Relationships
- Religion

- Reviews
- School and Studying
- Self-help
- Sewing, Knitting, etc
- Speaking
- Social Networking
- Spirituality
- Sports
- Teaching
- Technical
- Teens
- Travel
- Tweens
- Web Development
- Weddings
- Women
- Writing

# Samples of Work, Links & Special Projects

Providing samples of your work is absolutely essential for any writer's website, but especially for those who freelance. In fact, samples may be the most important component on a freelancer's author site.

It may seem obvious, but most potential clients will want to see samples of your work before they hire you—and thanks to the Internet, most would prefer to see them before they even speak to you.

The unfortunate fact is that no matter how fabulous you are, your well-put-together site (without samples) will often be overlooked in favor of a less qualified writer with a less fancy site (that offers samples.) There are several ways you can offer writing samples to your website visitors.

## Links

Set up a dedicated links page. On this page, you can create a detailed link list. Include links to any (or selected) online articles, columns or stories you've written, links to your blog(s), links to client sites and/or any other work you've published online.

Next to each link, write a brief description of why you're directing your client to it—how you are or were affiliated with the site or information about the work specifically.

For example, here is the text from two links on my own author website:

**The WM Freelance Writers Connection**--Angela and her partner Alyssa Ast founded the WM Network. Their first project was this comprehensive resource for freelance writers, which focuses on the business of writing and related topics. Today, the blog features seven different freelancers and has an online community group for its readers.

**In Pursuit of Fulfillment**--Angela's personal development blog, which focuses on fostering positive self image and taking charge of one's life through intentional choices and perception.

If you don't want a dedicated links page, or if you want an additional way to display your links, you can place them in your sidebar as a simple list.

## On Site Work

If you're not a blogger, you should become one. Every writer needs a blog. But if you're not ready to link your blog to your website yet, or if you don't have any work yet published online, you still have options.

You can make your work samples available on your website directly. You can do this in a couple of different ways. Perhaps the simplest way is to publish it directly on your website. You can do this in blog form, or you can create separate pages for your work samples.

Alternatively, you can offer downloadable documents for potential clients who want to check out your work. The downside to a downloadable document is that less people are likely to take the time to download it—after all; a click is much faster and less "invasive."

## Special Projects

A special project can be almost any kind of writing or writing related activity that doesn't fit into a different category. You might include things like group blogs, guest posts, interviews you've conducted (or interviews with you)—anything that could feasibly showcase your writing ability, or which would otherwise indicate expertise in a writing related area. For example, if you tutor inner city kids in reading, that could be considered a special project. Or if you are the founder of a blogging network or the organizer of a local writing group—well, you get the idea. Any writing related (or even writing adjacent) activity can be listed under "special projects" or a similar title.

## A Little Advice

Some writers, especially those who aren't yet familiar with online publishing, worry that their samples will be stolen. Therefore, these writers only offer samples by request. While this may seem like the safest option, and while you may be less likely to actually have your work stolen this way, it is also the least attractive to potential clients.

And remember, anything you send via email can ultimately be forwarded anyway—so technically, it's not much safer than putting your work out on a website.

Take appropriate precautions when offering unpublished samples of your work, like offering downloadable copies in read-only PDF files instead of Word documents, or by copy protecting your website. Back up all of your original documents and drafts, in case you should ever need to prove that your work is, well, yours.

Beyond that, most freelance writers just need to be vigilant and focus on running their businesses. And for a little extra protection, sign up for Google Alerts (a free service.) Then, set up alerts for your name, website name, blog title, articles, etc. This way, you'll be notified by email each time one of those items is mentioned and indexed as a newly published item, and you'll know if someone is publishing your work online without permission.

# Your Author Site Blog

A blog is, in its simplest form, an online journal. In fact, the term comes from early internet lingo–a slurred, shortened form of the phrase "web log." Bloggers generally post journal style entries or short articles, often containing links to other relevant websites, blogs or resources.

## Benefits of Putting a Blog on Your Author Site

Besides being a super-easy way to provide writing samples for potential clients, a blog on your freelance writer's website offers several other benefits.

**Search Engines Will Be Your Friend**—Probably the most notable benefit of an on-site blog is that it keeps your author website "fresh" in the eyes of the search engines. So, as you write and publish new blog posts, the search engines pick up each post. And, since blogs are typically content-rich, they tend to rank higher in the search engines—so they can help to increase your page rank and placement on SERPs (search engine results pages.)

**Establish Yourself as a Niche Expert**—Another benefit to having a blog on your author site is that you can use it to establish yourself as an expert in any given niche or topic area. For example, a writer who wants to establish himself as an editor might create posts related to proper writing techniques, grammar, spelling, punctuation and the related topics. A writer who wants to establish herself as a parenting expert could post about raising kids, while a writer who wants to focus on corporate accounts should direct blog posts to that end. You get the idea.

**Talk Yourself Up**—An author site blog is an ideal place to make announcements about projects you're working on, books you're writing and articles or stories you've published. Anything related to your writing career, really. Not only does it give you easy content, but it also shows your potential clients that you're continuously growing in your craft and your career. Plus, you can promote your work by giving yourself some much needed link love.

### Tips for Successful Blogging

Whether you're using it to market your services, to build a social platform or to establish yourself as a niche expert, you want people to read your blog (even if just to help boost your search engine rankings.)

It's easy enough to create a blog—and, if you're really passionate about your topic (or about writing in general), it might even be easy to create your posts—but many writers find that the easy part ends there.

Since the ever-expanding blogosphere has reached more than 126 million blogs (as of January 2010), the competition is fierce. So how do you get people to read your blog?

**Read and Comment on Other Blogs**—It sounds almost too easy, but one way to get noticed is to notice other bloggers. Find blogs that you enjoy reading, and especially those that focus on topics related to yours. Subscribe to and follow them, and then actually read and comment on their posts. In most cases, they'll return the favor (and their readers might click your link too.) Plus, you'll begin to develop a strong community feeling with your fellow bloggers. Spend a couple hours each week reading and commenting on other blogs, and watch your numbers soar.

**Stick to the Plan**—While an occasional off-topic post won't kill you, a blog that wanders too much might turn off your readers. Try to define and stick to a basic topic "umbrella." So, if you write about crafting, don't stick a cell phone review in there--but you could write one on a crafty app you have on your phone. Consider your target readers and stick with topics that might interest them.

**Interact With Your Readers**—Respond to comments left by your readers, and check out their blogs if they leave a link. Readers like to know that there's a "real person" behind the blog, and when you respond to and interact with them personally, they're more likely to come back and read your next post.

**Optimize Your Posts**—Using SEO in your blog posts can help encourage the search engines to pick up your content. Another benefit of using SEO for blogging is that it can help you to generate post ideas—you can write about what people are searching for (and want to read) in relation to your topic. WordTracker offers an easy-to-use, free keyword tool that works well. SEO is discussed in more detail in Chapter 11.

**Post Smart**—Provide high-quality, original and regular posts. They don't have to be long--anywhere from 150 to 500 words is an ideal length for a post. You can post daily, bi-weekly, week-ly--whichever works for you--but post on a consistent schedule whenever possible. Most blogging systems will allow you to set up posts in advance to automatically publish at a specified time and date, so you won't be chained to the computer when you're otherwise engaged. Not only will your readers appreciate the regularity, but the search engines will be more likely to pick up your content if you post on a consistent schedule.

**Email Subscriptions**—Sure, RSS readers are all the rage, and you should definitely offer an RSS feed. But also consider offer-ing email subscriptions to your blog. This way, readers can receive your posts or updates directly in their email box. While they may not click on every post, it will keep your name fresh in their minds, and you'll end up with more loyal readers. Google's Feedburner offers a free, easy to use and easy to set up email subscription service.

**Social Networking**—If you're not already there, it's time to get involved in social networking sites like Facebook, LinkedIn and Twitter. In the case of every social network, don't just blindly plant links and expect to get hits out of the deal. For positive results, you need to actually participate in conversations and genuinely involve yourself. Social networking is discussed in more detail in Chapter 13.

# Being Accessible

So, you've designed the Most Awesome Writer Website ever. You've got a killer blog, perfect writing samples, beautifully written and positive testimonials, and an expansive list of services—but without appropriate contact information, you've really got a whole bunch of nothing. If a potential client can't easily contact you, he will just move on to the next site, taking his business (and your would-be income) with him.

That's why you need to make it as easy as possible for the client to contact you quickly and easily. So what are the best types of contact information to include on your contact page?

**Email Address**—Put your email address front and center on your contact page, and hyperlink it so the client just has to click, type and send. If you're worried about spiders or bots picking it up, just type it like this: writer at writersite dot com, or hyperlink the address within text, like "Email Me" or something similar.

**Facebook Page**—Here's a (yet another) good reason to create a Facebook fan/like page. You can include a link to this page on your website. This way, potential clients, fans and friends alike can easily connect with you via Facebook so you'll stay fresh in their minds—and your personal profile can stay private.

**LinkedIn Profile**—Include a link to your LinkedIn Profile so that potential clients, business associates and fellow freelancers can connect with you there. LinkedIn is an amazing resource for freelance writers for many reasons, and many corporate clients would prefer to connect with you there.

**Twitter Account**— Include a link to your Twitter profile. Twitter is an ever-growing and sometimes overlooked (at least in the case of contact pages) social networking platform. Most every business has a Twitter account, and many prefer Twitter for its brevity and ease of use—especially folks who are often on the road and who tweet from their phones.

**Phone Number**—Some freelance writers like to include their telephone numbers on their websites, and some clients like to be able to pick up the phone and call for a quote rather than waiting for a response to an email. For a freelancer, this is a very personal choice, especially since she is likely to work from home—at least some of the time. In general, most freelance writers don't put their phone numbers on their websites and have no trouble finding business—and those who do put one up generally have a dedicated business phone. If you decide to put up a phone number, consider getting an 800 number which routes to your own phone, or a separate business line. You can even just add a cell phone to your personal account for around ten bucks a month with most providers.

## About Contact Forms

Many writers think contact forms make them appear more professional, but clients often find themselves frustrated and annoyed by them. Freelance writing guru (and author of Make a Living Writing: The 21st Century Guide) Carol Tice advises skipping the contact form and including a direct email address or link instead.

"Filling out forms is annoying, for a start, so that's not the first contact you want with a prospect. And prospects want to email you from their own platform, so it stays in their email archive and they can track the conversation," Tice says. "Also, when you fill out an online form and press send, the message disappears, and then visitors wonder if that technology really worked, and if anyone's really going to read it."

And, hey, if you're married to the form idea, just include your email address as well.

## Turn Around Time

Along with your contact information, you need to let your potential clients know how long it will take you to respond to their inquiries so that they know what to expect. And then, of course, you need to actually respond within the specified window of time.

In most cases, allowing yourself "one business day" to respond is sufficient. Business days are Monday through Friday, excluding national holidays. If you want to offer a speedier response—set up your author site email address to forward to your phone so that you can instantly reply even when you're not in front of the computer. Alternatively, you can set up an automated response which would automatically email your clients when they email you from the site, something like:

*Thank you for your inquiry! I will be in touch shortly to discuss your project.*

*Sincerely,*

*Jane Writer*

If you find yourself inundated with emails or super busy with clients, just change your response time on your contact page to something more feasible—maybe three or five business days. But don't make them wait too long, because you may not be the only freelancer they're contacting. If someone else beats you to the punch, you could lose potential business (and income.)

# 9

## Choosing a Hosting Service

If you don't yet have an author site, or if you aren't satisfied with the one you've got, you have a number of options when it comes to web hosting services. If you're building your site yourself (and you're not secretly a professional web developer or designer on the side) you can absolutely still create a website that will serve your business and your clients well.

While there are hundreds of different options for web hosting service for an author site, the following is a list of a few well-known, affordable (free or very low cost) and easy to use choices.

## Blogger.com

### *The Pros*

Blogger.com is owned by Google. You can create a blog for free, and with recent upgrades, you can also easily set up as many as ten dedicated (static) pages for your blog. You can also see the site's stats directly on the dashboard—including things like number of pageviews on each post, traffic sources and more.

Blogger is also one of the more flexible free blogging platforms. Not only does it include a custom designing "what you see is what you get" (WSIWYG) platform that almost anyone can use, but you can also upload your own custom HTML of you choose. And even if you don't write all the code yourself, you can incorporate blocks of custom HTML into a predesigned template, so you can include nearly any widget you like.

The Blogger interface is simple to use and there is a large body of troubleshooting information available online if you need help, as well as active forums.

Plus, Blogger is host to a large and supportive community of active bloggers—so putting your author site under the "Blogger" umbrella can offer instant exposure, especially if you're kind enough to read and comment on others' blogs.

You can also remove the "Blogger toolbar" at the top of your site. And, while your free Blogger URL will look like this: http://yourname.blogspot.com, you can purchase a custom one (http://yourname.com) for only ten dollars (USD) annually. Hosting stays free.

### *The Cons*

Blogger does not currently allow site owners to tuck their blogs into a tab—so your landing page MUST be your blog. While this isn't the worst thing in the world, some freelancers find it too restrictive and prefer other web providers for this reason.

Another downside: you can only import a blog's contents from another Blogger blog—not any other format. Also, without an upgrade, you only get one gigabyte of storage (though most don't have a problem with that.)

## Wordpress.com

### *The Pros*

Wordpress.com also offers a fairly easy to use interface (though many beginners say Blogger.com is simpler.) But unlike Blogger.com, Wordpress.com allows you to import blogs from nearly any other blogging platform (including Blogger, Live Journal, Vox.com, Movable Type, Posterous, Type Pad, Yahoo! 360 and other Wordpress blogs.)

Wordpress.com also offers three gigabytes of storage for free users, and if you need more space, you can pay for an upgrade. An upgrade also offers you the ability to upload more file types, like .ppt, .doc, .odt and .pdf. Plus, you can password protect certain blog posts or pages if you like. This could be an effective tool if you want to create a "clients only" area of your site, though most freelancers don't find this necessary.

You can also choose from a wide variety of Wordpress-friendly widgets, including a custom HTML block, meaning you can use nearly any widget on your site.

*The Cons*

You cannot edit a template or use a custom HTML template on a Wordpress.com site. If you choose to upgrade to a paid package, you can edit the CSS (style sheet) only—though some of the predesigned templates (more than 100 available at the time of this writing) do allow you to upload a header image and some offer additional customization options.

Along the same line, Wordpress.com does not support scripts of any kind, so you can't install third party tracker scripts as you can on other sites.

While Wordpress.com does allow you to create dedicated (static) pages within your site, they are listed in separate menus by default.

And, while Blogger offers free hosting with a purchased custom URL, Wordpress.com requires a paid upgrade to map a custom domain.

## Weebly.com

### The Pros

If you are totally clueless about web design but you want a custom author site, Weebly may be the way to go. You can choose from just under 100 different pre-designed templates, and you have the ability to edit the CSS and the HTML files, so customization is possible, though not simple.

The drag-and-drop design interface is attractive to those who aren't comfortable with the technical stuff—and it's easy to place various elements in one of Weebly's templates. Weebly also features the custom HTML box so that you can add outside widgets to your site. It's super easy to set up a website with Weebly.

Plus, Weebly offers you a dedicated landing page and allows

you to tuck your blog into a tab, which seems preferable for most author sites. You can even host more than one blog on a single Weebly site.

Weebly also offers reasonably priced custom domain names and add-on packages and has decent support. And, unlike other similar services like Webs.com, which places large banner ads on its free sites, Weebly only places one advertisement on free pages (removable with upgrade)—a simple one line link at the bottom which reads "Create a free website with Weebly." Far less intrusive.

### *The Cons*

Weebly's interface is very specific and quite restrictive, and there are certain custom coding adjustments that must be made if you try to upload your own HTML and CSS for the template. It can prove frustrating for many writers, especially those who dabble in HTML design.

Also, Weebly does not support sidebars, except within the blogging platform. This means that your blog text is narrower and looks a bit awkward in comparison to the other pages, and that the sidebar widgets are only visible if you've got the blog page open.

## Private Hosting With Wordpress.org CMS

*The Pros*

The Wordpress.org CMS (content management system) is free blogging software. If you use this software in conjunction with a site powered by a private web hosting provider, you can upload custom HTML and CSS through your provider's FTP, and therefore can completely customize and control every element of your site.

You can have a dedicated landing page, a blog tucked in a tab, multiple dedicated (static) pages, the widgets of your choice and more. You can re-order your pages to your heart's desire, and if you don't want to design your own template, you can choose from a large selection of predesigned Wordpress templates.

While this kind of website can be a little more technically involved than other options, if you can do it, you'll love the complete control you have in the design and maintenance of your author site. You can even upload your own plugins.

Once you've set up your template, the familiar and simple to use Wordpress interface becomes your control center—it's where you can work with your widgets and plugins, create blog posts, edit pages, moderate comments and more. Plus, unlike

Blogger and other platforms, you can actually edit your comments.

### *The Cons*

Going this route can be a bit more costly. You can usually find a decent web hosting service starting at just under ten bucks a month, and most bill quarterly, bi-annually or annually. And, as previously mentioned, you need more technical knowledge to set up and run a privately hosted site.

Some writers don't like that they have to download the Wordpress.org software in order to use it (whereas other providers maintain the software online.) Plus, you'll need to handle your own backups and manually upgrade to new versions of the software (while with other platforms, the software is automatically upgraded.)

Another thing: if your site develops a spam infestation, you're on your own, while other set ups offer spam protection. (But if you set up your comments to always be moderated, you can at least catch the problems before they're published on your site.)

## Bottom Line

When all is said and done, choose a service that works for you. Consider your technical abilities, your budget and your business needs and go with the service that meets your needs. You can always switch services later if you aren't satisfied with the one you choose. Also, if you do choose one of the free options, consider waiting to upgrade to a paid plan until you've decided you're satisfied with the capabilities of the platform. Don't get yourself stuck in a long contract if you aren't sure it's going to work for you.

# 10

# Pimp Your Author Site

After you've put together all of the content for your website and chosen a hosting provider, it's time to consider the layout and design of the site. Plus, you'll want to consider which kinds of widgets and other functionalities you want to incorporate into your pages.

The fact is that amazing content is only a part of what visitors find attractive about websites—the layout and design matters too. If it's not friendly or makes site visitors feel frustrated or confused, they'll click away and you could lose potential business.

### Tips for Successful Website Layout and Design

**Complication Free**—When it comes to your layout and design, keep it simple. It should be easy to use and navigate. Your potential clients should not have to dig around to find the information they need—instead, keep the site clean and clearly define the navigation. A top menu and/or prominent sidebar link-list are always safe bets.

**Friendly Fonts**—Even though you might love the pretty font that looks like cursive writing, it's hard to read, and many browsers won't support it. Stick to basic fonts for your main copy, and be sure to size it at no less than 11 pixels (though 12-14 is desirable in most cases.) Also, be sure to use appropriate spacing between text lines (12 pixels or more) to avoid a squished look.

**The Color of Success**—When it comes to your freelance business site, you obviously want to keep it professional and make it pleasing to the eye. The colors you choose can have a dramatic effect on your potential clients. A few tips:

1. Yellow backgrounds cause eyestrain. If you want to incorporate yellow, use it as an accent rather than a main template color.

2. Black backgrounds are also hard on the eyes, and limit your choices with text colors.

3. Stick to standard web colors which will appear the same

on every browser.

4. If in doubt, a white background with a simple black font is always a safe choice.

5. In any case, to achieve a professional look, consider using a simple palette with no more than two to four coordinating colors.

6. Consider the psychology of your color choices. For example, a contrasting palette of orange and blue can feel like excitement to your website visitors. A palette of more related colors like green and blue can feel positive and encouraging.

**Video**—While freelance writers don't always have much call for a video, some like to put a video introduction of themselves and their services on their website. And, if you also place your video on YouTube and your social networking sites, it can mean additional exposure for your site.

**Downloads**—Many freelance writers find success with downloadable documents designed specifically for their target clients. For example, you could offer a whitepaper that focuses on a topic that would be of interest to your client, such as a brief tutorial on SEO or social networking.

## Widgets and Plugins

There are thousands and thousands of choices for website and blog widgets and plugins, and since most web providers offer you the ability to insert custom HTML blocks into your template, the possibilities are virtually limitless.

While not even remotely all-inclusive, the following is a list of a few tools that could prove helpful to most any author site.

**Google Analytics**—Google Analytics is a very valuable (and free) tool that can be incorporated into any webpage that allows for custom HTML coding. Through Google Analytics, you can find out which of your marketing techniques are working (and which aren't,) where your website visitors are actually coming from (search words, referral sites, etc.,) which keywords work and which don't, which content people are most interested in, and much more. Effective use of the Google Analytics toolbox can significantly increase your site's success.

**Feedburner**—Another free tool from Google, Feedburner gives you the ability to offer email subscriptions for your blog. As previously mentioned, many people prefer an email subscription to an RSS feed subscription. Feedburner also offers many other benefits, too. First, you can set up profiles for each of your blogs, and you can customize each one. Feedburner even lets you see your subscribers list (which other systems don't always offer.) Plus, Feedburner gives you the option to create headline animators (to display rotating headlines,) the option to republish your feed as HTML, the ability to auto-publish to your social networks, access to some of your Analytics information, and much more. You can customize nearly every element offered by Feedburner as well.

**LinkWithin**—This tool is quickly gaining popularity with bloggers. The primary function of the LinkWithin widget is to show related stories (along with thumbnail photos) at the bottom of each blog post. This kind of widget can increase your visitors' time on your site, and encourage additional clicks—thereby potentially increasing your site ranking. Plus, it's a great way to help breathe life into your old stories, especially for new site visitors. LinkWithin is very easy to use and install, and works with any site that allows custom HTML blocks.

**ShareThis and ShareIt**—ShareThis and ShareIt are similar services which offer your site visitors the option to share your content on social networks or through email with just a click. You could also choose to put individual icons for sharing in your favorite social networks, but with tools like ShareThis and ShareIt, you can be sure that most everyone will be able to use it with ease since they feature so many different options. Both services listed here are easy to use and install, so long as you are able to add the custom HTML blocks to your site.

**FeedJit**—If you're an instant gratification kind of person, Feed-Jit is for you. With the free FeedJit widget, you can watch your site traffic in real time. This means that as people arrive on your site, you can see where they're logged in from and where they go once they're on your site—whether it's to an internal link or an external one. And, with FeedJit Pro, even more details are available. One caveat: some writers don't like the look of the widget, and you have to put the widget on your site in order to use the service.

**Badges**—Social networking (like Facebook and Twitter) badges in the sidebar can encourage additional followers and more direct interaction with potential clients.

**SEO Plugins**—Most website and blog platforms offer their own SEO plugins, which can help to maximize your site's exposure by helping to optimize your content for search engines. For example, WordPress offers a free "All in One SEO Pack."

# 11

# SEO for Your Author Website

SEO stands for Search Engine Optimization. It's essentially the process of creating content and enhancing the layout and design on your website to attract the highest number of visitors possible through various search engines.

In layman's terms, SEO is a constantly evolving science which focuses specifically on making your website more search engine friendly.

Since SEO makes your website more attractive to search engines, it has the potential to draw in new readers who often become customers and referral sources. Researchers estimate that around 90 percent of first time visitors arrive on websites via search engines like Google and Yahoo. And, the more often your site is visited, the more the search engines like it.

## How SEO Works

Search engines "crawl" the web with automated programs called spiders or bots. Research indicates that approximately half of the more than 20 billion existing pages have been crawled.

Web pages which have been crawled are then indexed by the search engines, so that when web users type their search terms into one, it can quickly determine which pages in that index are relevant. Search engines each have unique algorithms to choose which pages show up and in what order they appear.

So why should you care about any of this? Studies show that most people will click on the results nearest the top of the search page. So, to put it simply:

*Optimizing Your Website=Higher Search Engine Rankings=More Clicks=More Traffic=More Potential Customers Viewing Your Content*

## Using SEO to Optimize Your Author Site

Once you understand the concept of SEO, it's simple to incorporate it into your author site.

Alyssa Ast, SEO/SEM expert and author of "The Fundamentals of SEO for the Average Joe" offers this advice for optimizing your author site with SEO:

Utilizing SEO within an author website is essential for marketing yourself as a writer. Strategically placing the keywords/phrases needed to optimize an author website is vital for traffic success.

To put it simply, incorporating the ideal keywords/phrases within your site, along with the proper keyword density, increases the likelihood that clients and readers will visit your site. When optimizing an author website, you must remember to update your site with new keywords/phrases regularly to maintain a steady flow of traffic.

Choose a short tail key phrase (a key phrase that contains 2-3 words with a maximum of 3 words) to use for the titles of your web pages. This is essential for success because the title of a web page will be that page's URL, and shorter URLs statistically result in more traffic. This key phrase, along with the other keywords/phrases you choose to use, need to be incorporated within the web content at a key word density level (the number of times keyword/phrases appear within web content compared to the full content word count) of 4% to 5%. You also need to include the keywords/phrases within the Meta description and Meta Tags section as well to successfully rank high on SERPs.

**Finding SEO Keywords and Phrases**

Keywords and key phrases are the terms that people type into search engines to find the information they need. When someone is searching for a freelance writer, they might type in "freelance writer" or "help with writing," for example. If they need help editing, clients might type in "editing services" or "proofreader."

And, many clients who prefer to work locally will type in the name of a city or regional area. (So be sure to include your general location in your Meta description, at the very least, if you're interested in working locally as well as globally.)

In general, choose key phrases of 2 to 4 words. In addition to simply checking search engines like Google and Yahoo to find hot topics and trends and to determine which websites are competing with yours, you can use a keyword research tool. One free and easy to use option is Wordtracker's free keyword suggestion tool (which can be found at http://freekeywords.wordtracker.com.) Wordtracker also offers a paid subscription with more benefits, but the free keyword tool is sufficient for many writers.

Simply type in your intended key phrase and a list of similar popular search terms will appear. You may then choose the keywords or phrases that fit best with your site from the list.

Choose keywords that have a "hits number" (the number of times the word or phrase has been typed into a search engine on a given day) of no more than 10 or 12. This way, you're competing with less websites (using the same phrase) and have a better chance of ranking higher on the SERPs.

For your author site, you might type in terms that describe the services you offer—writing, editing, genre name, etc. Get creative!

*Tip: remember that search engines index every page of your site individually, so add SEO keywords and/or phrases to each page to ensure that your site is most efficiently optimized.*

## A Word of Warning

One issue to consider when using SEO on your author site: many writers are so focused on making their material search engine friendly that it doesn't flow properly. This makes the writing seem stilted and unnatural–and hard to read.

Don't only worry about search engine optimization when you're putting together the copy for your website. Otherwise, while you may get a few extra clicks in the beginning, you'll find that you develop a high bounce rate since readers aren't interested in nonsensical and useless information. And, most search engines take this into account–meaning that the more often a reader lands on your page and immediately clicks away, the lower your website's search engine rank and SERP placement can fall.

The writing needs to flow naturally and be reader friendly— so write your copy first and then incorporate the SEO words into it.

The fact is that your potential clients are intelligent people– and if you post substandard articles and other low value content on your website just for the sake of SEO, people are bound to question your credibility.

Present your clients with well-written, interesting and easy to read content, and they're far more likely to stick around and find out what you and your business are all about.

# 12

## Advertising on Your Author Website

These days, there are all sorts of ways to monetize websites. Many options require very little set-up, just a bit of simple HTML coding (which is conveniently provided for site owners by advertisers or affiliate organizations.)

It's a very personal decision, but it helps to know what you're getting yourself into if you choose to advertise on your author site.

The most obvious "pro" to advertising on your website is the possibility that you'll make money doing so. And, if you select advertisers that sell relevant products or services, your site visitors probably won't mind, so long as ads are simple and static.

Many writers refuse to place any advertising, outside of their own services, on their author sites. Their logic is that advertising on their sites can negatively affect their credibility as a writer, or they worry about what potential clients will think if they see advertising on the site.

## Types of Advertising

While there are hundreds of different methods used for website advertising, the following are some of the most common utilized by freelance writers on their websites.

**Pop-Up Ads**—Pop-up ads are exactly what they sound like—advertisements that open when a site visitor clicks or moves their mouse cursor on a certain part of your webpage. Pop-up ads and those which impede the site visitor's experience by requiring them to click to close the ad are annoying and may also cause the page to load very slowly or even crash on some browsers and systems. Many potential clients will click away to a competitor's site when these types of ads are used.

**Real Estate**—If you simply choose to sell "real estate" (a spot in the sidebar, for example) on your site, you can charge a one-time, upfront fee to run the ad for a specified amount of time. If your site gets enough traffic, advertisers will be interested in purchasing a piece of your success. And, when the specified advertising time is finished, many advertisers will renew the contract to continue to run the ad on your site. A word of advice: avoid ads which involve flash or other types of animation to minimize your page loading time. Besides promoting your own services, this is a preferred method of advertising for author sites (if you choose to advertise outside of your own brand.)

**Affiliate Advertising**—There are many different affiliate advertising programs available. These kinds of programs generally involve either a spot in your sidebar which links to a specific site or product, or pre-determined links within your content. If the affiliate advertiser's product or service is compatible with your platform (and is not a direct competitor), you can, in most cases, successfully incorporate the ads or links into your site. Just like with SEO, though, you'll want to be sure the ad flows naturally with the rest of the page. One good example of an effective affiliate advertising campaign for writers is Amazon Associates, which allows you to choose the books and products that are advertised on your site.

**Links for Pay**—Some organizations allow you to list your site and encourage advertisers to contact you directly to arrange links and ads. Blogsvertise, for example, allows writers to register their blogs for the perusal of advertisers. Then, the advertiser uses the Blogsvertise system to contact blog owners and offer a certain dollar amount for text links or ads. Generally, advertisers pay a one-time flat fee for this kind of advertising. One pro here is that this kind of advertising is unobtrusive in most cases—but a con is that the payment average is pretty low.

**Interstitials**—Interstitial ads are shown when a website visitor clicks on an internal link (one which goes to a different page within the same site) during the transition from one page to the next. Use this type of advertising with extreme caution because it's not only annoying, but can also increase your site's load time, making it far less user friendly. Most people agree that in addition to pop-ups, interstitials are among the most irritating kind of online advertising.

**Sponsorships**—Lucky freelance writers sometimes obtain corporate sponsorship for their blogs. This means that a specific sponsor (or group of sponsors) will pay the site owner to integrate their ads into the site on a more global basis—and when done properly, these types of advertisements are subtle and effective. While this is perhaps the most effective way to monetize your site, corporate sponsors don't often approach freelancers to sponsor their sites. Still, some bloggers have found great success with this type of advertising.

**Your Other Websites/Ventures**—Maybe the most acceptable form of advertising on an author website is the advertisement of the author's own websites, blogs, books or products. Include links or badges for your social networking accounts, your blogs and/or any other website affiliation you might have.

# 13

## Social Networking & Site Promotion

Now that you've created, designed, optimized and filled your freelance writer website with useful content, it's time to start promoting it—and promoting yourself in the process.

Thanks to the technology we have today, the world of social networking makes it easier than ever to promote yourself and your work—and for free.

### Let's Talk Statistics

Early in 2010, Facebook reported that at least 50 percent of active users log in to their Facebook accounts every single day. This means that more than 250 million people hit the Facebook site every 24 hours—and the number is ever growing.

Around the same time, Twitter reported that it had 75 million user accounts—though a "mere" 15 million were active on a daily basis. And, Twitter reported, the "average" number of tweets per day was nearly 30 million at the end of 2009.

LinkedIn reported in Feburary 2010 that it had around 60 mil-lion users, and in December of 2009, it reported that membership had soared by 5 million accounts in the previous two months.

Americans who use the internet spend about a quarter of their online time on actively engaging with social networking sites, according to a Nielson research report. On average, that's around 6 hours each month. And, the report says, an additional 36 percent of online time is used to communicate and network across blogs, social networks, instant message and personal email. This, of course, includes many of your potential website visitors and clients.

Clearly, the possible benefits of promoting yourself within the social networking platform cannot be ignored. Still, there are some unspoken rules to consider when you go this route.

**Think Before You Submit**

Ever felt really frustrated and banged out a tweet or Facebook status in a fit of rage, only to instantly regret it and hit the delete key? You're not the only one.

Still, even if you instantly delete the tweet or status, once you hit that "submit" button, it's "out there"—meaning that someone might have seen it or otherwise be able to find it.

Many editors and potential clients are likely to Google you be-fore they hire you. How do you think they'd feel if they no-ticed your tweet last week about that crappy client you finally dropped? Or the one about the argument you had with your spouse? Most likely, it would negatively affect their opinion of you or your abilities.

As a general guideline, don't ever do or say anything on the Internet that you don't want your potential clients to see or hear—because chances are that if you do, they'll see it—and that can hurt your bottom line.

## Actively Network

A lot of people just don't "get" the whole social networking thing. You can't just blindly plant links on these sites and expect the payoff to come rolling in. You must actually and genuinely participate in the communities that are involved, or you might as well not even bother.

Read and respond to other people's comments and posts. Inte-ract with them—have ongoing meaningful dialogue. Don't be afraid to help your fellow writers out—they can be some of your most helpful networking resources.

And don't just network with other writers—get involved with business owners, friends, family members, PR agents, editors—friends of these people—any and everyone you can. You never know who could turn out to be a great referral source or other type of valuable resource.

## About Automation

It's ok to automate some parts of your social networking efforts, but do so sparingly. For example, using the free Facebook application called Networked Blogs, you can auto-post your blogs to your personal and business walls. This is very handy and a big time saver—but you still need to watch the posts and respond to comments from your friends and fans.

Using another free service called Social Oomph, you can automatically follow back people who follow you on Twitter, and even set up an automatic direct message (DM) to thank them for following (among many other features.)

One way to get them to interact with you through an auto DM is to ask a universal question—like "What's your favorite book?" or "Tell me more about you!" Of course, the same rule applies—once they respond to your auto DM, you'll need to acknowledge it and reciprocate personally.

Remember: people don't want to communicate with an automated system—they want to communicate with a real live person. Use automation to your advantage, but do so with appropriate caution—and don't completely remove the human element. Your network isn't going to build itself.

### Spam Sucks

Don't spam people. Post your links on social networks appropriately—don't fill someone's Twitter timeline or Facebook newsfeed with the same post over and over again.

And, the occasional special circumstance (your first published article, the announcement of your book release, etc.) might war-rant a mass email, but don't send emails to everyone in your address book every time you publish a blog post or article.

Instead, employ the use of your onsite blog and a basic subscription service—this way, those who want to know the details of your career can "opt in" and you can post your news on your site blog.

## Site-Specific Etiquette Tips

**Facebook**—Share links to your blog posts and online articles with your friends, and put a link to your author site and blog in your profile. You can also set up a Facebook Fan Page (a "Like" page) for yourself (the freelance writer,) your blog or author site, or both. As previously mentioned, Facebook offers a free (and useful) application called Networked Blogs which will automatically share your blog posts with your friends and fans via your blog's RSS feed.

**LinkedIn**—There are countless active interest groups on LinkedIn. You can find writers' groups, career specific focus groups, family and parenting groups, lifestyle groups and more. After you've created your LinkedIn profile, join groups that might be interested in your blog posts, and submit links to the groups' news sections or news subgroups (unless the group's rules specify otherwise.) Involve yourself in the discussions of your blog posts as well as those that other members post.

Note: While LinkedIn groups can be amazing referral sources, don't spam in any case, don't submit links to unrelated groups, and be sure to read and follow each group's posting rules. Generally, you need to start a discussion that does not require group members to click your link in order to participate in the discussion.

**Twitter**—Follow people who have interests that are related to your blog topic and your business, as well as potential clients or referral sources, and they're likely to follow you back. People who show more "follows" than "followers" are a good bet because it usually means that they "follow back." Spend some time reading, responding to and re-tweeting other people's tweets each day, and they're likely to do the same for you when you share your links. Customize your profile to match the theme of your site and to gain more interest.

# 14

# Other Ways to Promote Your Author Site

While social networking sites provide an excellent (and free) option to promote your freelance writing business website, many writers find success with other forms of promotion as well. After all, the more self-promotion you do, the more opportunities you'll have to gain new clients and raise your income.

Now it's time to get creative and come up with new and unique ways to drive traffic to your site—and potential income to your bank account.

Here are a few ideas to get you started.

## Business Cards

Every freelance writer needs business cards, and you can get really nice looking ones for next to nothing from a service like VistaPrint. In fact, VistaPrint also offers free business cards (if you don't mind a small advertisement on the back.) You can even print them out yourself, but if you don't have a high-quality printer and cardstock, the cards won't look as professional.

Be generous with your business cards. Carry them with you all the time, and pass cards out to anyone who will take them— and give a couple to business associates, friends or family members who might be able to refer potential clients. Leave some at your local chamber of commerce or business association. Drop them in shops around town—send them along with manuscripts and business proposals. You get the idea.

Keep the design basic and professional. Don't get too complicated or outrageous, unless that's the image you're shooting for.

Include your name, title, website address, email address and telephone number, at the very least. For example, here's a black and white version of my business card, minus the telephone number:

You can also utilize the back of the card to give more information about your services. Here's the back of my card:

## Freelance Services

*Reporting *Non-fiction Articles *SEO *Web Content
*Creative Writing *Ghost Writing/Blogging *Press Releases
*Corporate/Management Documents *Newsletters
*Editing Services *Speech Writing *Social Networking
*Company Image Development *Workshops

## Specialty Topic Areas

*Business *Legal *Medical and Health Insurance
*Health and Fitness *Family & Parenting
*Women's *Personal Development *Motivational

**Online Advertising**

In addition to the promotion you do on social networking sites, you can place free ads on sites like Craigslist and Yelp.

Plus, you can list yourself in a number of different freelance writing databases and on freelance writing websites. Many writers report success with this kind of advertising, but if you go this route, remember that there are no regulations in place and you may have to weed out a few crazies. Use appropriate caution when dealing with any new client.

You might also find some success in trading links with other writers and bloggers—at least on some level. Though some writers aren't interested in sharing links with the competition, many are supportive of their fellow writers—especially when the benefits are mutual. For example, if one of your "extra" services is editing and your colleague offers book formatting, you could each link to the other's page by specifically citing those services.

### Print Publications

Magazines like Writer's Digest have classified sections where many writers and editors (and other industry professionals) choose to insert paid ads. You can do the same with local news-papers and business publications. While this kind of advertising is far less common and can get quite expensive, the return can be worth the investment, especially for a high-quality freelance writer. (And don't forget—high-quality and experienced are not always the same thing.)

## A Word of Encouragement

For many freelance writers, the idea of promoting themselves is pretty intimidating. Especially when you're new to the business, you might worry that because you're inexperienced, people won't take you seriously—or that they'll find reasons criticize you or your work. Some new freelancers even feel a bit like "frauds" or "posers" when they first begin to promote their work, since they haven't been published in any significant markets yet.

Let's face it—there are no hard and fast educational requirements or other regulations when it comes to "being a freelance writer." Anyone can call himself a freelance writer—but not everyone can be successful in that role.

Here's the thing you need to remember. If you are passionate about writing and you love your work, you will be successful. So what if you have trouble with commas or can never remember whether you should use that apostrophe when using the contracted form of "it is?" Make it your mission to learn the things you need to learn to be a successful writer.

If you really want to be a writer, you're a writer. The next step is to become a professional writer so that you can be paid to do something you love doing. A professional writer is defined as a writer who has been paid for their work. So technically, this means that even a writer who has been paid one dollar to publish an article on a content site qualifies as a "professional."

And one last thought—don't be afraid to show your work to family and friends. It may feel awkward at first, but most often, you'll find that their praise and support helps you to feel more comfortable promoting yourself to the world.

# Appendix: Resources for Freelance Writers

## Websites

- Absolute Write: http://absolutewrite.com/
- All Freelance Writing: http://allfreelancewriting.com/
- Amazon Associates: https://affiliate-program.amazon.com/
- BlogCatalog: http://www.blogcatalog.com/
- Blogger: http://www.google.com/alerts
- Blogsvertise: http://www.blogsvertise.com/
- Christina Katz ~ Empowering Writers: http://christinakatz.com/
- Copyblogger: http://www.copyblogger.com/
- Feedburner: http://feedburner.google.com/
- FeedJit: http://feedjit.com/
- Funds for Writers: http://www.fundsforwriters.com/

- Google Alerts: http://www.google.com/alerts
- HARO (Help a Reporter Out):

http://www.helpareporter.com/

- JMR Web Information and Technology Support and Services (Web Hosting): http://www.jmrweb.net/
- LinkWithin: http://www.linkwithin.com/
- Make a Living Writing:

http://www.makealivingwriting.com/

- Mediabistro: http://www.mediabistro.com/
- Mike's Writing Workshop:

http://mikeswritingworkshop.blogspot.com/

- Networked Blogs: http://www.networkedblogs.com/
- Online Writing Jobs: http://www.online-writing-jobs.com
- Poe War Writing Career Center:

http://www.poewar.com/

- ShareThis: http://sharethis.com/
- Social Oomph: http://www.socialoomph.com/
- Surefire Writing: http://www.surefirewriting.com/
- The Freelance Writing Jobs Network:

http://www.freelancewritinggigs.com/

- The Purdue Online Writing Lab (OWL):

http://owl.english.purdue.edu/

- The WM Freelance Writers Connection:

http://wmfreelanceconnection.com

- VistaPrint: http://www.vistaprint.com/
- WeBook 911 Writer's Block:

http://www.webook.com/911writersblock

- Webs.com: http://www.webs.com/
- Weebly: http://feedburner.google.com/
- Wordpress.com: http://wordpress.com/
- Wordpress.org: http://wordpress.org/
- Wordtracker Free Keyword Tool:

http://freekeywords.wordtracker.com/

- Write to Done: http://writetodone.com/
- Writer Beware: http://www.sfwa.org/for-authors/writer-beware/
- Writer's Digest: http://www.writersdigest.com/
- Writer's Villiage University: http://writersvillage.com/
- Writers Weekly: http://www.writersweekly.com/
- Writing Careers Examiner: http://www.examiner.com/x-48681-Writing-Careers-Examiner
- Writing Job Resource: http://writingjobresource.com/

## Books

- *Bird by Bird* by Anne Lamott
- *If You Can Talk, You Can Write* by Joel Saltzman

- *Make Living Writing: The 21st Century Guide* by Carol Tice
- *My So-Called Freelance Life: How to Survive and Thrive as a Creative Professional for Hire* by Michelle Goodman
- *On Writing* by Stephen King
- *On Writing Well* by William K. Zinsser
- *The Anti 9- to -5 Guide: Practical Career Advice for Women Who Think Outside the Cube* by Michelle Goodman
- *The Artist's Way* by Julia Cameron
- *The ASJA Guide to Freelance Writing*
- *The Associated Press Stylebook*
- *The Chicago Manual of Style*
- *The Elements of Style* by Strunk and White
- *The Fundamentals of SEO for the Average Joe* by Alyssa Ast
- *The McGraw-Hill Handbook of English Grammar and Usage* by Lester & Beason
- *The Renegade Writer: A Totally Unconventional Guide to Freelance Writing Success* by Formichelli & Burrell
- *The Well-Fed Self-Publisher* by Peter Bowerman
- *The Well-Fed Writer* by Peter Bowerman
- *The Well-Fed Writer, Back for Seconds* by Peter Bowerman
- *The Writing Life* by Annie Dillard

- *Writer's Digest Handbook of Magazine Article Writing*
- *Writer's Market*
- *Writing Down to the Bones* by Natalie Goldberg
- *Zen and the Art of Writing* by Ray Bradbury

## Groups & Associations

- American Crime Writers League: http://www.acwl.org/
- American Society of Journalists and Authors (ASJA): http://www.asja.org/
- Asian American Journalists Association (AAJA): http://www.aaja.org/
- Australian Society of Authors: http://www.asauthors.org/
- Canadian Authors Association: http://www.canauthors.org/
- Critiquegroups.com: http://www.critiquegroups.com/
- Electronic Literature Organization: http://www.eliterature.org/
- Military Writers Society of America: http://www.militarywriters.com/
- National Association of Independent Writers and Editors (NAIWE): http://naiwe.com/
- National Association of Science Writers (NASW):

http://www.nasw.org/

- National Writers Association (NWA):

http://www.nationalwriters.com/

- National Writers Union: https://nwu.org/
- National Writers Union: https://nwu.org/
- Native American Journalists Association:

http://www.naja.com/

- Pennwriters: http://www.pennwriters.org/
- Small Publishers, Artists and Writers Network

(SPAWN): http://www.spawn.org/

- The American Society of News Editors:

http://www.asne.org/

- The Association of Young Journalists and Writers:

http://ayjw.org/

- The Authors Guild: http://www.authorsguild.org/
- The International Women's Writing Guild:

http://www.iwwg.com/

- The Internet Writing Workshop:

http://www.internetwritingworkshop.org/

- The WM Freelance Connection Online Community:

http://groups.google.com/group/The_WM_Freelance_Connectio

n

- Writer's Guild of America: http://www.wga.org/

- Writer's Guild of Canada:
http://www.writersguildofcanada.com/
- Writers Café: http://www.writerscafe.org/
- ZoeTrope: http://www.zoetrope.com/

# About the Author

Angela Atkinson is a freelance writer, editor and researcher. She has been writing since she could hold a pencil and is passionate about the craft. The nineties found her writing for her high school and college newspapers and yearbooks, and later a small regional magazine.

Atkinson currently writes and edits content for several websites and various private clients. She also does basic website construction and design, social media marketing and social networking on behalf of her clients and is an SEO expert.

She writes an award-winning personal development blog called In Pursuit of Fulfillment, which focuses on living well and personal development.

Along with fellow freelance writer Alyssa Ast, Atkinson founded The WM Network. The WM Network currently includes four resource websites, including The WM Freelance Connection, The WM Parenting Connection, The WM Pet Connection and The WM Review Connection.

Atkinson studied journalism at Eastern Illinois University and has been a full-time freelance writer, editor and researcher since 2005. She lives in St. Louis, Missouri with her loving husband and three amazing children.